J 745.5
Turnbul P9-EGB-475
Diaries and keepsakes :
style secrets for girls

$28.50
ocn833374796
04/04/2014

GIRL TALK

DIARIES AND KEEPSAKES

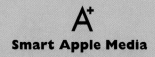

Style Secrets for Girls

STEPHANIE TURNBULL

A⁺

Smart Apple Media

Published by Smart Apple Media, an imprint of Black Rabbit Books
P.O. Box 3263, Mankato, Minnesota 56002
www.blackrabbitbooks.com

Library of Congress Cataloging-in-Publication Data

Turnbull, Stephanie.
Diaries and keepsakes : style secrets for girls / Stephanie Turnbull.
pages cm.—(Girl talk)
Includes index.
Summary: "A fun magazine-like book for preteen and teen girls on crafty ways to make
and keep memories of events. Includes information on decorating, writing in, and
hiding a private diary. Also includes idea for using photos to create scrapbooks
and other photo keepsakes, such as mugs"—Provided by publisher.
Audience: Grades 4-6
ISBN 978-1-59920-945-6 (library binding)—ISBN 978-1-62588-996-6 (ebook)
1. Handicraft for girls—Juvenile literature. 2. Book design—Juvenile literature. 3. Diaries—
Juvenile literature. 4. Gift books—Juvenile literature. 5. Scrapbooking—Juvenile literature. I. Title.
TT171.T875 2014
745.593'8—dc23

2012051570

Created by Appleseed Editions Ltd,
Designed and illustrated by Guy Callaby
Edited by Mary-Jane Wilkins

Picture credits

t = top, b = bottom, l = left, r = right, c = center

title page Christopher Halloran/Shutterstock; 2t Aleksandr Bryliaev, b artzenter/both Shutterstock; 3t Studio DMM Photography, Designs & Art, inset kostudio/both Shutterstock; 4 Ilike, b Africa Studio/both Shutterstock; 5t badge James Clarke, teddy Milos Luzanin, flag Annmarie Young, postcards bepsy, snowglobe MarFot/all Shutterstock, medal Guy Callaby, l Hemera/Thinkstock, stamp catwalker/Shutterstock.com, b Stephen Chung/Shutterstock; 6 diaries: heart-shaped sagir, blue Gabriel Nardelli Araujo, red spillikin, leather pio3, hands holding book Tatiana Popova, diary with post-its schab/Shutterstock, b nuttakit/all Shutterstock; 7t ueapun, r Adrian Hughes, b folders Hong Vo, punch and cards ben44, tags Paul Gibbings, ribbon WitthayaP, paperclips Elena Blokhina/all Shutterstock; 8tr Jo Ann Snover, t Rob Hyrons/both Shutterstock; 10tl Begum Ozpinar, r & c Raymond Kasprzak, teapot bookmark Cousin_Avi, open diary Pedro Nogueira, bl sagir, br Nata-Lia/all Shutterstock; 11 Victoria Brassey/Shutterstock; 12 doodles JeremyWhat, stars ildogesto, faces Murat emir colcu, b Cheryl Casey/all Shutterstock; 13c holbox, l Kiselev Andrey Valerevich, cr mojito.mak[dog]gmail.com, notepaper happydancing/all Shutterstock, r Neftali/Shutterstock.com; 14t lkphotographers, r Ints Vikmanis, b Baronb/all Shutterstock; 15t Lamella/Shutterstock, c iStockphoto/Thinkstock, r & b vovan, pen jedka84/all Shutterstock; 16t DNF Style, tent Serg Zastavkin, girls and camera irina.roibu, girl with hat cabania, three girls dotshock, girls on beach oliveromg, l Andi Berger/all Shutterstock; 17t Anatoliy Samara, sunflower frame Santiago Cornejo, photo inside Samuel Borges Photography, roses frame Dmitri Mikitenko, dog JulijaSapic_Portfolio, bead frame Dr Ajay Kumar Singh, hijab girl Zurijeta, orange frame Brooke Becker, tug-of-war oliveromg/all Shutterstock, b iStockphoto/Thinkstock; 18 waiter iStockphoto/Thinkstock, stamp Neftali/Shutterstock.com, metro sign iStockphoto/Thinkstock, sign Julian de Dios/all Shutterstock, Eiffel Tower iStockphoto/Thinkstock, ticket AKaiser/Shutterstock, old stamp Halima Ahkdar/Shutterstock.com, cl jan kranendonk, c aldorado/both Shutterstock, b waiter, Rue de Croissant, Eiffel Tower from boat/all iStockphoto/Thinkstock, bow trekandshoot, envelope alien-tz/both Shutterstock; 19 br hole punch Bara22, scissors tetyana radchenko, bl Alexandr Makarov/all Shutterstock; 20t kuleczka, l crazycolors, b Hannamariah/Shutterstock; 21 sledge girl Smailhodzic, r Snaprender/all Shutterstock; 22 pegs and line Jag_cz, girl and dog Nuzza, Muslim girl ansar80, girls on bench Olesia Bilkei, b girl winking Timofeeva Maria, frames Archipoch/Shutterstock; 24t Catherine Murray, l Fuse/both Shutterstock; r & b iStockphoto/Thinkstock; 25b Ysbrand Cosijn/Shutterstock; 26tr boomerang Ashwin, coathanger R. Gino Santa Maria, coloured pencils Jordi Muray, pot Tramont_ana/all Shutterstock, b iStockphoto/Thinkstock; 27t book ene, ticket Olga Kovalenko, sellotape Shane White/all Shutterstock, ribbon iStockphoto/Thinkstock, map Brand X Pictures/both Thinkstock; 28 MANDY GODBEHEAR/Shutterstock; 29r Patrizia Tilly, b Hank Frentz/both Shutterstock; 30b Sharon Day/Shutterstock; 32 Uli Eckardt/Shutterstock
Front cover: OtnaYdur/Shutterstock

Printed in the United States at Corporate Graphics in North Mankato, Minnesota.
PO DAD5005a
102013

9 8 7 6 5 4 3 2

Contents

4 All About You

6 Choose Your Diary

8 Cool Covers

10 Diary Decorations

12 Start Scribbling!

14 Private – Keep Out!

16 Fantastic Photos

18 Scrapbook Basics

20 Stylish Scrapping

22 Creative Displays

24 Storage Solutions

26 Think Practical

28 Making Memories

30 Glossary

31 Smart Sites

32 Index

All About You

Think about all the things that make you unique—your ideas, memories, interests, and goals. Writing in a diary and surrounding yourself with special things is a great way to express yourself. And it's fun!

Dear Diary...

Diaries are perfect for recording important events and experiences, or just to have a good rant and get something off your chest! Writing down feelings, fears, or worries can make you feel better—and jotting ideas, lists, or plans keeps you organized.

Magical Memories

Keepsakes are objects that remind you of special times, people, and places. They might be gifts, photos, collections, prizes, or well-loved toys. Whether they're priceless **heirlooms** or cheap souvenirs, the point is that they are precious to YOU.

Be selective with your stuff. What's important and what's just junk?

Pssst... Hot Tip!

Look out for these tips throughout the book. They give you all kinds of extra advice and ideas for creating special diaries and displays.

Fun Diary Facts

One of the earliest diaries was written in the 2nd century by a Roman Emperor named Marcus Aurelius.

DEUTSCHE BUNDESPOST

ANNE FRANK · 12.6.1929 · 31.3.1945
1979

Possibly the most famous **diarist** ever was Anne Frank, a Jewish teenager whose family hid in Amsterdam during World War II.

Nowadays, many people compose online diaries, or **blogs**, which can be read by friends – or complete strangers!

Choose Your Diary

Diaries come in all different shapes and sizes. They may be huge, thick journals with space for detailed descriptions of each day, or slim pocket books for brief notes and quick lists. So, which one is right for you?

Diary Types

First, decide if you want to write a daily account of your life or only occasional entries when something really interesting happens. A tiny, dainty diary is no use if you run out of space. At the same time, having a vast, empty page to fill every day could be daunting!

You can always clip or tape extra pages in your diary.

Pssst... If you don't like writing by hand, use a computer, but be sure to back up your work regularly – it would be terrible to lose everything!

Pick and Choose

Remember that diaries don't have to cover an entire year—how about keeping a vacation journal, or writing a summary of each week, month, or school year? You could also **review** movies you've watched, books you've read, or places you've visited.

Neat Notebooks

It's often better (and cheaper!) to buy a good notebook instead of a diary. This lets you write as much or little as you want, whenever you want. Start each entry on a new page and remember to put the date at the top.

Packs of small notebooks don't cost much and always come in handy.

Make Your Own

If no diary or notebook is quite right, create your own. Punch holes in paper and tie them together with **treasury tags**, ribbon, or yarn. You could also write on computer paper and file them in a ring binder, or help the environment and recycle scrap paper.

Be creative and use lots of bright, cheerful colors.

Cool Covers

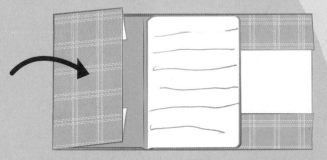

A beautiful cover transforms an ordinary book into a special journal that you'll enjoy writing in! Try one of these clever cover ideas, using colors and designs that reflect your personal style.

Smart Jackets

Here's a neat way to make a simple jacket using paper, gift wrap, or wallpaper. Swap it for a new one whenever you want!

1. Cut a piece of paper 2 in (5 cm) bigger than your open diary at the top and bottom and about 5 in (12 cm) wider at each end.

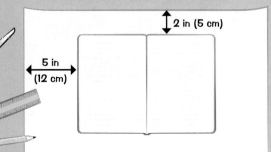

2 in (5 cm)

5 in (12 cm)

3. Place the open diary in the center of the folded paper. Wrap the left end of the paper over the front cover and crease at the edge.

2. Crease the paper at the top and bottom edges of the diary, then move the diary out of the way and fold the paper neatly along the creases.

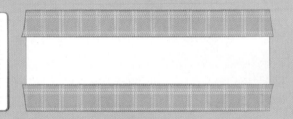

4. Now slide the front cover into the sleeve you've created.

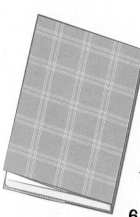

5. *Shut the diary and wrap the other end of the paper over the back cover. Fold in and crease along the edge.*

Don't leave the book open, or your finished jacket will be too small.

6. *Slide the back cover into the sleeve.*

7. *If you want, decorate with stickers, pen doodles, or pictures cut from magazines.*

Funky Fabric

Make a fashion statement by dressing up your diary! You'll need an old shirt with a front pocket.

Pssst... Kids' shirts are ideal for this as the pockets are small.

1. *Lay the shirt and diary face down, with the pocket in the middle of the cover and the edge of the shirt lined up with the diary edge. Draw around the diary.*

3. *Lay the material in place and tuck in the long, cut edge so it doesn't fray. Keep it in place with craft glue or a few stitches.*

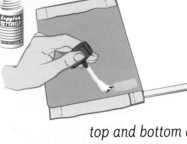

4. *Spread glue over the front cover and stick on the material. Glue the top and bottom edges inside the front cover. Allow to dry, then cover the back in the same way.*

2. *Carefully cut along the three sides about 1 in (2 cm) outside the lines you drew.*

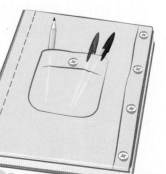

5. *Use the front pocket as a handy place to store pens!*

9

Diary Decorations

You can decorate your diary with much more than just a cover! Try these ideas for all sorts of imaginative extras to make your diary one of a kind.

Bling It Up

Give your diary some glitz by gluing on gems or sequins, and hang keychains or charms from the rings of spiral-bound books. Make a fancy fastener by threading beads on thin elastic, tying it in a loop, and stretching it around the diary to keep it firmly shut.

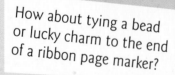

How about tying a bead or lucky charm to the end of a ribbon page marker?

Ribbon Markers

Some diaries and notebooks have ribbon page markers attached, but if yours doesn't, tape a ribbon to the inside back cover—or weave one up through the loops of a spiral-bound diary and leave the end to hang inside the book.

Another method is to loop ribbon through a paper clip, then pull the ends through the loop. Attach your clip to a page.

Make several ribbon clips to mark different pages.

Pssst... Stick decorated envelopes inside your diary for storing odds and ends, such as photos or secret notes.

Perfect Pens

Once your diary looks fab, you'll want a beautiful pen to go with it! Colorful pipe cleaners are great for livening up plain pens and pencils. Coil them around the end and add extra decorations...

... or fold one in half around strands of yarn...

... then thread on a few beads...

...and wrap the pipe cleaner around the top of your pen!

Start Scribbling!

So you've got your diary and you're ready to write—now get started! Here are some helpful tips to keep you motivated and make sure you don't give up. Remember, the more you write, the more important your diary will become.

Make Time

Diary writing has to be part of your regular routine if it's to become a habit. Set aside some time each day, perhaps in the evening after homework. If you're too tired by then, how about getting up ten minutes earlier in the morning to write?

Be Flexible

A diary isn't schoolwork, it's for YOU—so there are no rules about what to write! If you feel you must include every detail of your day, then diary writing will soon become a chore. Get straight to the important stuff and say how you feel about it.

Don't spend all evening watching TV! Set aside half an hour for diary writing.

Use stickers to express how good or bad your day has been.

Mix It Up

Your diary can be the place for everything that's going on in your head—ideas, opinions, dreams, poems, or wish lists. Jot down inspiring or funny **quotations**, useful recipes, or random facts. The more variety you include, the more interesting your diary will be to look back on later.

Sei Shonagon, a Japanese woman who lived 10,000 years ago, wrote a diary full of gossip, advice, jokes, and lists of likes and dislikes.

If you don't feel like writing about real life, why not have some fun and imagine you're a spoiled celebrity, rock star, or superhero?

"Tried on dresses for the Oscars. Can't decide between Versace and Chanel."

"Played my biggest gig ever tonight. Sold-out crowd, four encores."

The artist Frida Kahlo included sketches and paintings in her diary.

"Good day today. Rescued a planeload of people, foiled a bank robbery, saved the world. Took afternoon off."

Samuel Pepys, who wrote a detailed diary in the 1660s, described important events such as wars, plagues, and the Great Fire of London.

Pssst... Use your diary to analyze things that bother you and brainstorm solutions. Avoid being unkind toward other people.

Private ~Keep Out!

Your diary is personal and not for sharing—which is why nosy brothers or sisters would love to get ahold of it! Avoid this by writing in private and keeping your diary somewhere safe. Here are some more top-secret tips.

Sneaky Spots

Think carefully about where to hide your diary. Don't go for obvious places such as under the bed or in a drawer. If your diary is small and slim, make this crafty pocket.

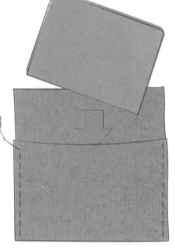

1. Wrap a large rectangle of **felt** over your diary.

2. Stitch the sides so the diary can slip in and out easily.

3. Tape your secret pocket to the back of a picture or wall mirror…

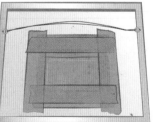

… or sew it on to a coat hanger, then cover it with clothes.

Fold the top flap over the hanger and stitch in place.

Clever Camouflage

Disguise your diary as a dull school notebook so that nobody will give it a second look. Stack it casually with text books and you can be sure it will never be read!

Which would be most tempting to open? This…

MATH PROBLEMS

…or this?

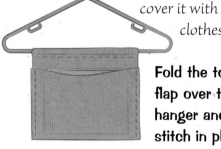

PRIVATE DO NOT READ!

14

Codes and Symbols

Writing in code protects private information, but it takes time, so you may not want to do it every day. Many codes substitute letters of the alphabet for a symbol or another letter.

Dictionary Codes

Grab a big dictionary (with more than a thousand pages) and try this brilliant code—it's fiendishly tricky to crack and doesn't use a written **key** that someone could find.

Ancient Egyptians used pictures to signify certain things. You could try this too.

1. Look up the word you want and write down the page number. Make the number four digits long by adding zeros in front, if necessary.

2. Now write 1 or 2, depending on whether the word is in the first or second column, then count down the entries in that column and write the position of your word. If it's a single digit, add a zero in front.

disaster

(first column, second entry)

0368102

368
(page number)

3. Do the same for each word to make a series of 7-digit numbers, meaningless to everyone... except you.

0368102 – 0780212
0879122 1005209!

(Disaster – lost my phone!)

Pssst... If you don't mention that you keep a diary, then no one will search for it.

Fantastic Photos

Photos are often the best kind of keepsake. They bring back great memories instantly, perhaps of important days, fabulous vacations, or people you love. Displaying photos prevents them from getting lost or crumpled, and you can admire them whenever you want.

Photo Albums

One obvious place to put photos is in an album. Choose one with large, self-adhesive pages so you can arrange your photos freely and stick them in place easily. You could also buy **corner mounts** and place photos into scrapbooks.

Think Smart

Albums are expensive and fill up fast! Squeeze in extra photos by overlapping them on the page, making sure you don't cover the important parts.

Clever Cuts

Another way to save space is to crop photos. In other words, cut out sections you don't need. Don't slice off too much or you won't be able to tell where the photo was taken.

Pssst... Try cutting around people or objects to create unusual photo shapes.

Fab Frames

A frame is a great way to display a favorite photo, by hanging it on the wall or standing it on your desk or bedside table. Choose a style and color of frame that suits your image, or decorate a plain wooden frame by gluing on buttons or shells.

You can also frame certificates, posters, or even T-shirts.

Photo Facts

The first permanent photograph was taken in 1826 in France. The photographer had to leave the camera undisturbed for eight hours before developing the picture!

Hand-held cameras became popular around 1900, and were bulky and box-shaped.

Digital photo frames store hundreds of images and display them in a slideshow.

Scrapbook Basics

Pssst... Why not put together a scrapbook as a thoughtful gift for someone special?

To make photo albums more interesting, why not add tickets, letters, and other souvenirs to create a scrapbook? If you don't want to fill a whole book, design individual pages to frame or keep in a ring binder. Here's what you need to start scrapbooking.

School Trip to Paris: Day 1

Plan Each Page

Before you affix anything permanently, plan your scrapbook carefully. Each page needs a theme, so give it a title, then decide what to include. Use both photos and mementos.

Don't cram in too much – if you have several similar photos, pick just one.

Remember that you can crop photos (see page 17) to save space.

Now plan your layout. Start with one large, important element, then position everything else around it. To make things stand out, try mounting them on a card in a **contrasting** color and overlapping them at a slight angle.

Glue things in place when you're happy with the design, then add captions, labels, or notes.

Now turn the page for more advanced scrapbooking ideas and techniques!

School Trip to Paris: Day 1

This is from the bonbons Ethan gave me. (!)

Our waiter looked a bit like this!!

Emily checks the map yet again...

Scrapbook Snippets

The earliest scrapbooks date back to the 16th century, when girls wrote, drew, and placed pictures in books called friendship albums.

Modern scrapbooking became popular in the US in the 1980s. Today, millions of people make scrapbooks.

Serious "scrappers" use **acid-free** paper, ink, and glue, plus special tools, such as wavy-edged scissors and fancy hole punches.

Stylish Scrapping

There are many clever ways to give your scrapbook a professional look. Here are a few to try—but don't use them all at once, or your pages will be too busy!

Glam It Up

Small decorations, called **embellishments**, are useful for filling gaps and adding extra dazzle. You can buy these from craft stores but the cost soon adds up, so try making your own. For example, tie a bow from a scrap of lace or ribbon, cut paper flowers, or sprinkle on glitter.

Rough and smooth

Create interesting texture combinations by layering thick, grainy paper on shiny gift wrap, or tear paper rather than cutting it to make a rough, unique edges.

Torn strips of paper make great borders for scrapbook pages.

Rip It Up

Here's another effective torn paper technique. Fold a piece of paper in half and draw a shape next to the fold.

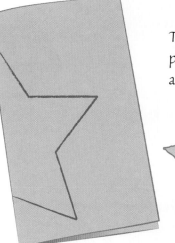

Tear around the line, then open up the finished product. Use the torn shape to mount a photo, and the rest of the paper to frame another.

Have Fun!

Scrapbooks are often filled with memories that make you smile, so have some fun with your layouts. A Halloween page might have googly eyes dotted over a black background, as well as silly ghost jokes under flaps. You could also give photos funny captions or even turn a sequence of photos into a comic strip.

EXCLUSIVE FROM THE WINTER OLYMPICS

Just watch this!

WHEEEEEEEEE!!!!!

World sled champion poses for the photographers

WHOOOOOOSH!!!!

SPLAT!!

Okay, you can stop watching now...

(Think I need more practice...)

Finishing Touches

Don't spoil a great design with messy, smudged handwriting! Choose good-quality pens and write slowly and neatly, or make letters with stencils instead. Use a computer to create titles and captions in all kinds of fancy **fonts**.

Pssst... Give photos extra impact by sticking small squares of foam or cardboard on the back to raise them off the page.

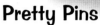

Creative Displays

Filling your room with favorite photos and mementos is a great chance to use your imagination and have some fun. Here are some brilliantly easy ideas for really inventive displays.

Artsy Arrangements

If you have space, put photos in several similar-colored frames and arrange them on the wall in a neat interlocking design. If you prefer something less precise, tack up snap after snap until you've covered the wall in one enormous **photomontage**!

Pretty Pins

If you're short on wall space, why not clip photos, cards, and other keepsakes with clothespins? Use plain wooden or plastic clothespins, and paint or decorate them however you want. String up some yarn, ribbon, or Christmas lights, and hang the clothespins from it.

How about taking one big picture and framing it in sections, like this?

Covered Cork Boards

Cork boards are handy for displaying paper mementos—but the pins leave holes in your memorabilia. Avoid this by making a stylish cork board cover with fabric and ribbon.

1. Put the cork board inside a pillowcase and push it to one corner.

Choose a color or pattern that matches your room decor.

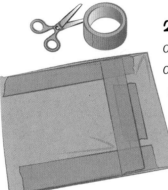

2. Fold the edges of the pillowcase over the back of the board and stick them down with strong tape. Stretch the fabric tightly.

3. Cut a length of ribbon long enough to cross the board diagonally. Hold it in place with push pins on the back.

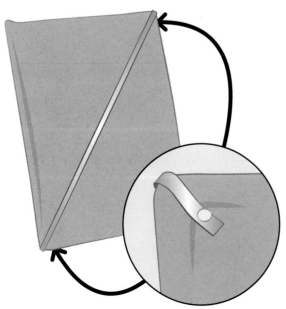

4. Put more lengths of ribbon across the board, then repeat in the other direction to make a diamond pattern. Press a tack into each ribbon intersection.

5. Slide photos, tickets, letters, postcards, and other odds and ends under the ribbon.

Pin a loop of ribbon on the back to hang your board.

Pssst... Ask an adult for help when hanging frames or cork boards.

Storage Solutions

Keepsakes are often treasured collections. You can collect anything—dolls, stuffed animals, figurines, keychains, buttons, tickets, badges, erasers . . . you name it! Whatever your collection, it should be stored safely and arranged attractively.

Only collect things you love—don't just copy your friends.

Hooks are ideal for bags, skates, and other mementos that can be hung up.

On Display

Shelves, bookcases, and windowsills are obvious places to display candles, jewelry boxes, and other large objects, while glass cabinets keep things from collecting dust.

Cool Containers

Small items such as beads, coins, or stickers may be best kept in boxes, jars, or tins. Thrift stores are perfect places to find unusual and attractive containers, while clear plastic boxes are useful if you want to see what's inside.

Handy Pockets

To store odds and ends, make felt pockets like the one on page 14 and decorate them. Cover a cork board with fabric (see page 23) and pin your pockets to it.

Use cheerful, bright thread.

Sew on beads, buttons, felt shapes, or bows.

Decorated Tins

Give a cookie tin a stylish new look by covering it with glossy pictures. This is called **découpage**. Choose images that suit your theme. For example, sea creatures to cover a tin of shells.

1. *Cut lots of images from magazines. Mix some craft glue with a little water, so it's runny.*

2. *Spread glue over the lid and sides, then cover with pictures, brushing each with glue as you stick it down. Allow to dry.*

Overlap pictures and don't leave gaps.

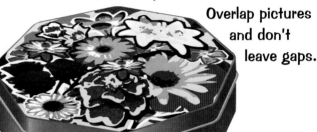

Pssst... For a glossy finish, paint on a layer of clear nail polish—but do it near an open window as the fumes are strong!

Crazy Collections

Some people have huge collections of ordinary objects such as spoons, tea bags, traffic cones, and bags of chips!

A special "gnome reserve" in Devon, England displays the world's largest gnome collection—2,042 in total.

Stamp collecting is one of the most popular hobbies ever. In 2011, one rare stamp sold for more than $1,600,000.

Think Practical

There's a limit to how many keepsakes you can display before your room becomes cluttered! Give some precious mementos a practical purpose so they're useful rather than gathering dust.

Why not fill a clay pot with pencils? Or reuse that souvenir boomerang as a coat hanger?

Photos Galore

It's easy, and fairly cheap, to have photos printed on a variety of things including keychains, clothes, mouse pads, phone covers, bags, calendars, and more. Look for photo services in large supermarkets or online.

Get photos of friends printed on mugs. These also make great gifts!

Brilliant Bookmarks

Tickets are the perfect shape for bookmarks. First, mount them on durable cardstock.

Make more bookmarks by cutting cards, photos, or maps into strips. Add decorations, such as ribbon, then stick wide, clear tape over the bookmark to protect it.

T-shirt Pillows

Don't fill drawers with old T-shirts too special to throw out—transform them into cute pillows instead! All you need is a needle, thread, and a soft filling, such as old towels, socks, or pillow stuffing.

Use thread the same color as the T-shirt so it doesn't show.

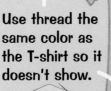

1. Turn the T-shirt inside out. Carefully sew up the arm holes and along the bottom. Use small, neat stitches to hold the material together.

2. Turn the T-shirt the right way and stuff it, pushing the material into the corners.

3. Seal up the neck hole by stitching the **seams** together.

More Pillows

Other kinds of clothes make funky pillows, too. How about experimenting with shorts or skirts? Turn vests inside out, sew straight across the top, then stuff and sew the same way as a sleeved T-shirt.

Pssst... A T-shirt pillow makes a sneaky hiding place for a finished diary. Push your diary deep inside the stuffing before stitching up the neck.

27

Making Memories

Looking back at old diaries and precious keepsakes is great fun—so the more you have, the better! Here are some hints and tips on how to keep creating fantastic memories.

Start Snapping!

It's easy to take photos with a camera phone, so take a few pictures whenever you're having a good time. But make sure you upload them to a computer or print copies in case you accidentally delete them.

Get Organized

You must be organized to create good albums, scrapbooks, and displays. Keep photos and other memorabilia in order and write the date, place, and useful information on the back. These details may seem obvious now, but in a few years you'll have trouble remembering!

End of school picnic, May 29 2013, Castledene Park.

Left to right:
Sam, me, Jo, Ellie, Sophie.

Pssst… The sooner you put photos and mementos into albums or scrapbooks, the more details you'll remember, and the more enthusiastic you'll be to include it all.

Go Out and About

If you want photos of fab parties, get a group of friends together. Be sure to include others you know would like to attend, and hey, why not ask someone who is new to school or maybe on the shy side? It's always great to make new friends!

Keep Writing

Stay in touch with long-distance friends or relatives by email, then print their replies. Also, keep any letters and cards you receive. Ask friends to send you funny postcards whenever they go on vacation!

Take photos of your family on special occasions or days out.

Start a **family tree** and hunt for fascinating old photos.

Glossary

acid-free
Without the natural acids that make materials gradually discolor and fall apart over time.

blog
Short for "web log," an online diary that often allows readers to add comments to entries.

contrasting
To be very different from something else. Pairing two contrasting colors can help each to stand out.

corner mounts
A small, self-adhesive photo corner. Slip one on each corner of your photo before placing them on the page.

découpage
The technique of decorating a surface with paper cutouts.

diarist
Someone who writes a diary, especially one which is then published.

embellishment
An extra detail or decoration added to make something look more interesting or beautiful.

family tree
A diagram showing information about members of a family and how they are related.

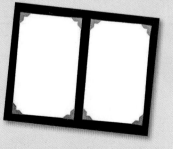

felt
Fabric made from matted wool. Felt is easy to cut, cheap to buy, and comes in lots of different colors.

font
A style of lettering. If you're using a very decorative font on the computer, make sure it can be read clearly.

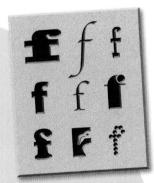

heirloom
Something that has been in a family for years, passed from one generation to the next.

key
A list of meanings of coded letters or symbols, or a clue to work them out.

photomontage
The technique of making a collage from photos.

quotation
A few words or a longer piece of writing, perhaps from a book or speech. Good quotations are funny, wise, or meaningful to you in some way.

review
To report on something (such as a book, play, TV show, or film), describing whether you think it is good or bad and explaining why.

seam
The place where two pieces of fabric have been sewn together.

treasury tag
A short string with a metal bar at each end, used to hold papers together.

Smart Sites

www.ehow.com/how_2161152_write-a-diary.html
Essential diary-writing tips, help, and advice.

www.artistshelpingchildren.org/journalsdiariescraftskidshowtomakediary.html
Artsy ideas for inventive and unusual diary covers and decorations.

www.wikihow.com/Create-Secret-Codes-and-Ciphers
How to create fantastic codes to use in a top-secret diary.

http://tlc.howstuffworks.com/family/picture-frames.htm
Lots of imaginative picture frame designs using all kinds of materials.

www.spoonful.com/create/scrapbooking-ideas-keepsakes-gallery
Fantastic scrapbooking ideas plus creative ways to display keepsakes.

http://tlc.howstuffworks.com/family/paper-desk-organizers.htm
Easy ideas for making desk organizers for your bedroom.

Index

beads 10, 11, 24, 25
blogs 5
bookmarks 27
buttons 17, 24, 25

captions 19, 21
charms 10
clothespins 22
codes 15
collections 5, 24-25
computers 5, 6, 21, 28
cork boards 23, 25
covers 8-9, 10
cropping 17, 18
cushions 27

découpage 25
diarist 5, 13
displays 5, 16, 22-23, 24, 29

embellishments 20
envelopes 11

fabric 9, 23, 25
felt 14, 25
fonts 21
framing 17, 18, 21, 22
Frank, Anne 5

hiding places 14, 27

Kahlo, Frida 13
keychains 10, 24, 26

letters 18, 23, 29
lists 4, 6, 13

magazines 9, 25
Marcus Aurelius 5
memories 4, 5, 16, 21, 28
mounting 19, 21, 27

notebooks 7, 10

page markers 10-11
pens 9, 11, 21
Pepys, Samuel 13
photo albums 16, 18, 29
photomontage 22
photos 5, 11, 16-17, 18, 21,
    22, 23, 26, 27, 28, 29
pipe cleaners 11
pockets 9, 14, 25
postcards 23, 27, 29

recycling 7, 26
ribbon 7, 10, 11, 20, 22,
    23, 27

scrapbooks 16, 18-19,
    20-21, 29
sewing 9, 14, 25, 27

shells 17, 25
Shonagon, Sei 13
souvenirs 5, 18, 26
stickers 9, 12, 24
storage 24-25

tickets 18, 23, 24, 27
T-shirts 17, 27

vacation 7, 16, 29

worries 4, 13
writing 4, 6, 7, 12, 13, 15,
    19, 21, 29

yarn 7, 11, 22